THESE THINGS TOO
HAVE SHAPE

WILLIAM STRATTON

Winter Goose
PUBLISHING
where words take flight

Winter Goose Publishing
45 Lafayette Road #114
North Hampton, NH 03862

www.wintergoosepublishing.com
Contact Information: info@wintergoosepublishing.com

These Things Too Have Shape

COPYRIGHT © 2016 by William Stratton

First Edition, January 2016

Cover Artwork by Mike Bourbeau
Typesetting by Odyssey Books

ISBN: 978-1-941058-05-3

Published in the United States of America

Contents

For Nana Ruth,
my most ardent critic and supporter

For my grandfather,
whose name I carry and whose presence I will not forget

Milkweed

For Jayce

I suppose some must go to twilight-lit Parisian streets,
to cities where mouths are open and the teeth inside
are more people. To great buttressed cathedrals
puncturing sky, blackening with time . . . but not me. Imagine
a hill near a farm whose farming is done and now only the house
and the foundation of a barn remain. On the side of that hill
which is still clover and orchard grass and timothy,
which still has the remnants of stone walls sliding every year
further into nothing . . . none of these things, but on that hill—
a patch of grass will not grow. There, a milkweed, gray, dead,
burst with seeds. That is my Paris.

No One Dances

Each night before sleep the man with three fingers plays
the mandolin and wishes for his missing digits back.
His left hand. His right is normal, and when he thinks
how he lost them he remembers the impossible shoulders
of the black horse and the white of its teeth, the spinning
shaft of the power take-off and the hum of the mower.
Each morning he fumbles with the laces of his boots
though it has been decades since the horse. Some days
the handle of his coffee mug slips and dances away, twirling
in the early sun, trailing its dark dress in an arc of frozen
air and he remembers then that the last time he had
all of his fingers he had a wife who bore him two sons
and she too whirled away, though the music that played
behind her flat eyes was consumption, and the ballroom
a ward full of white beds. No one ever danced for him
anymore. No one listened to him while he played, while he
moved his missing fingers over the long body and felt the
holes; each a reminder, a stab in the dark, the motion
of the wings of a bat in a dark room. Did I say it was
a mandolin? I was wrong. It was a harmonica, and his fingers
flipped and shimmied and the harp wailed and moaned
and even the cows turned to look.

What I Know of Killing

What there is to be heard—
usually in rattles, gasps, rasps,
or of a body in slowing motion
on whatever ground there is;

for me usually the tall, dead grass
and brown leaves and snow and each
having held one sound in particular
for just this moment, a sudden harsh rustle,
and then quite a lot of nothing—

is heard all at once and sticks with you
imperfectly, in such a way as you might
question if you had heard it at all;
was that a gurgle you might say
or had I stepped in mud or breathed
once from a deep place and forgotten,

or played the sound over again until
it had become something else,
the way the sound of children playing
becomes geese flying overhead, or
the passing of cars might become
the low murmur of conversation

in the next room. Nothing ever
forgives you for killing it, not even
things in great pain, as when I came
upon the deer which had lived more
than a day with a bullet in its belly
and without front legs, I saw only
fear and felt only pity, but a hard pity

of resignation, of knowledge and action
and I had to forgive myself for not
finding it sooner, or finding the man
who had done this to force a reckoning.
The deer did not thank me. In the last
seconds it tried to pull itself from the bloodied
pine needle floor and hump away.

Three Miracles

Today a storm carries dusk around its edges
and the brown sky sheds a frozen skin,
pushed east by wind until sunset pours
over iced trees and the smallest branches
shine like mirror balls. Snow grows
over the Atlantic and beaches cap white,
turning their backs, dragging the deep.

I found a wooly bear on the path
the snow-blower made between the door
and the car. Pulled from leaves, curling
sluggish on yellow grass. Moths do not know
about winter, about the cocoon cold can bring.

Just before morning I rose at the sound
of my father on the deck. He was
getting ready for work; I could smell coffee
and thought about what he might see from the window.
I had not sleepwalked in many years. I was grateful
to have smiled at him, to have seen him smile, to have
touched his shoulder before the stars of Orion's belt
and the cold broke through, and the spell was gone.

Eastern Bluebird

Heavy mower in the heat, three
acre yard, locusts and apples
and maples. Brown hands,
white palms, blue eyes. Stump
of a giant elm with a house
nailed to its side. "Come spring
he fought sparrow, swallow,
starling. Wore a hat so his talons
couldn't pierce my scalp." A man
must defend his home.

"Watched him every day in spring. Fought
like a bastard. Never quit. Swallows won,
sometimes." About failure: broken eggs,
turned-out nest. "Damned shame."

The maples have come down, the lilacs
no longer flower. "Pulled the stump
when I was twelve with a tractor
and chains. The house never came
off. They don't come no more."

Absence, memory, bluebirds. What is rotted
on the inside will hold us for only so long.

Nuthatch

In the golden leaves of forsythia another me is
reaching out his hand who might already know
about the nuthatch dancing nervously between
slender branches. Who might already have seen
what I will see around the next bend, have
a scar I do not, or a child, or explored some bit
of poem I have not yet found among the scattered day.

Much of my life is gone. The day is spent
and I cannot recall the touch of my wife
as she left for work . . . but I recall the forsythia.
I recall the nuthatch, and the tilt of its head as it
measured my speed and judged what distance it must
keep from me and thinking then about how its entire body
weighs less than one of my thick hands, about how
its hollow bones have allowed it flight. I wonder
how much of me must be hollow in order to rise
above the vinyl siding and slip from double-paned
windows to manicured backyards, and if I might
lie unnoticed in the grass as it regains color.

I have found myself in the first hours of light
which spring has added to evening
remembering the walk I have taken in the day.
In the lengthening afternoon there is the world
which lay all winter in the melted snow
now released to the creek. Hidden in the body of the man
I have not yet transformed into I have discovered
a kind of life I badly want. He too has seen it; I will remember.

Untitled

Those on the bridge hear:
walking over briny rivers
watching moon cast a burning net
into clouds and the current
pulling first towards mountains
then fleeing with bare trees,
un-anchored boats, the earth.

Everything is called. Moonlight
is only sun from the other
side of the world. Its halo
carves a crooked line on water.

From the bottom, voices
pulled from shells,
dragged from translucent
sea to blinding silt.

Estes Park, Colorado

It was September and hot and I lay on stiff hotel sheets
listening to the sounds of bull elk bugling and remembering
how I climbed all day and saw nothing but more mountains.

Every scream-grunt reminded me—I could have drowned
myself in the bathtub and the maid might not even have
whimpered, just turned and walked out, made her way

to the front desk; disturbed but together. The town would issue
me a paragraph in the weekly newspaper and in the morning
when most people are just waking for work old men at diner

counters would read and shake their heads. The temptation
plain enough for the waitress to see, in their muttering,
the call of something else beyond breakfast, and the next sip

of coffee would be bitter and lack comfort and all month
they would hear me in the bugles of the elk, fading into echo
and wind and then storms of winter and unlikely to return next fall.

What It Feels Like To Get Punched In The Face

First: surprise. The feeling of force, unexpected.
The transfer of kinetic energy, the movement

of a part of your body that your mind has not
ordered. A bright light sometimes, the blank screen,

early sun through the blinds of your bedroom,
and the sound in your head of a high pitched whine

and deep roar laid one on top of the other in such a way
as to make them the sound of many voices

all at once exclaiming. Warmth, heat,
the moment of realization, reaction, the mind

has caught suddenly what moment this is—
the moment in which someone else wishes

you harm, where all the people you have known
and places you have been are left behind and worthless,

and all of the rules you have followed are broken
down into nothing, because nothing matters then

but what happens, and words are meaningless sounds
and whatever it is you are seeing is only color and light
and the odd shapes of a dream. A snapping back,
the leash of reality catching your neck, focus.

Then pain.

Who Can Write In Spring

Cowslips raise yellow heads
and bow them again. Litter of autumn:
forget-me-nots. Ice gives way
to mud. A pair of geese disturb
the windless surface. The sky,
empty. How can it be eight years
since a pond like this held you in the big
blue truck until you died?

I did not cry; sitting while a small
snake basked beside me, or when I watched through
tilted blinds the evening put on its slow pursuance
for the western horizon. In the month of the longest days
I tread the careful water of missing you.

First Day of Trout Season

The two of us wrapping a cast-iron pan in newspaper,
packing matches and a stick of butter in the light before dawn.
Walking in the tag alder swamp casting side-arm,
watching the water for a strike. Watching
the water and knowing everything
about what was beneath—round stones, mud, roots.

Me, listening for my father in the new grass,
and later for fire and the sounds of fish swimming
in butter, and the morning as it grew late, and the wind.

The story of the bite, the struggle to land
the first fish, the story of its white belly
and the season as it changed with us,
the story of its hunger sating ours, and our story—
wading, silence, weaving, and loss.

The one where we caught the twelve-inch brookie,
where we were caught in a sudden storm, where we caught
nothing. We are still there, hooked along the cut banks,
snagged with crooked branches pulled together,
losing boots to the sucking swamp, the grab of brambles.
On the best days we break over the sides and rush with
melted snow, and though we have swallowed the fly
there will be another hand to free us, there will be
something we can feed together, a hunger which
the sacrifice of our bodies will spend itself on, and sate.

Prado

"Once in a while God takes poetry away from me."
—Adelia Prado

Waiting for the bus I take a few words
from the thorns brushing the glass stop. Half the year
they have no fruit or flower and hold out hooked
fingers to snag passersby like lonely children—*take me*
with you, take me to see the world, take me away.

Once in a while they keep just a spot of blood.
Now though, each tosses a green-red mane
as autumn sneaks into them. The hummingbirds
have all flown south and the people are untouched,
sitting with the first long sleeves of the season, waiting.
Once in a while one takes a poem away from God
and tucks it into a notebook, thinking *I look*
at a stone and see a stone.

What We Have Become

On the stage, men who know
they will never be famous. Women too,
crooning broken melodies and passing
their fingers over tarnished strings.

This is the last time
they will hear themselves
as small somebodies,
until next week.

Tomorrow one will lay wire
in the new development, another
will wait tables.

Take a look at their fingers, swollen
ankles, charcoal eyes. Tonight
each will put in their mouths
songs that make them,

for fifteen minutes among
beer and chatter, like the birth
of a god; raw, new, coming out
into a world full of others.

On the Bus to School

Ducks tuck their heads
in fog lifting from the river.

Frost leeches from the
dead leaves. A stone wall near
the bank runs out and up
the hill. I don't know to where.

Black water falls over the dam
and the finger of the bay creeps
in among houses. Its briny sides
rise and fall as the sea takes its breath.

I know the day will pull this longing
from me, but for now I am allowed
to miss these things even as they happen
around me. Ice falls from singing brakes;
people stand, the bus settles.

Ducks

The sluggish river now white and clouded,
and on it ducks staring miserably
at their un-paddling feet, preening

their un-wet feathers, watching
the likes of me, on the bridge,
wishing I had bread or corn to give
in recompense for the weather.

Do they know about the thaw?
They hope to keep away from
foxes long enough for water to lift
its dark head again.

Their dreams: the muddy blanket
beneath and what grasses grow
in the roiling spring.

Cat

I wanted to ride my bike a little before
the sun set but there on the road was half
a cat. Across the valley the sky furrowed
an orange-red brow and the last of July's
flowers let themselves be torn by wind
and I couldn't pedal on and just pretend
I hadn't noticed: the bits of it almost black
and the flies wheeling in delirious circles
back and forth towards the tall grass.
I risked the ticks and the wild parsnip
to get a good sized stick and lift her off—
I wanted her to know I had seen her
and thought to move her a little ways
towards home, towards the safety of
the darkness I know cats prefer, I wanted
her to know I would want that for me
and though she was just a cat I wanted
her to know I thought that was as much
a thing as I am, that we both could have seen
the summer as it pulled away from us
and headed west and south and on another
day we might both have made something
like a contented sound, we might both
have known what the other was in full,
and we might both have known a
fullness of our own because of it.

Fox

Pauses and turns, looks over her shoulder at me—
and I remember here is where I wanted to be all spring,
letting go of that which is not the fire of her body,

or sun through the canopy—
the meeting of our eyes
across this small clearing.
The rest of the morning
will ring with her absence

and when she returns
it will be her shape I dream of,
pulling this moment by the threads of itself
into her long red dress.

The Night My Mother Sang To Me

A thousand miles away I lay awake under mean desert stars
burnt through sky into the red rock. Sun seeped from the ground.
Above me night birds I did not recognize spilled black and hollow;
I saw how each made a part of the world disappear in a long feathered arc
and the sound they made: air cut into ribbons falling in slow curls around me.

I pleaded with them to stay, in case they had not heard
their songs were only songs, their wings only fingers
ending as frayed rope, their mouths like iris without end—
they could speak as things which cannot understand
that the opposite of lonely is alone, and ribbons, and song.

Barn Swallows, North Country

Mayflies spatter against hill fields;
each has broken promises—

that what goes up must stay forever up,
that flight is given to all creatures as a measure of breath,

that what has been wondered at will resolve.
The swallows call. It is the call of wolves,

the call of hunger, the call of promise.
What else could be said of what they do

in the air? Some dances begin and end with wind.
The summer evening pulls the light lengthwise

across the long grass, waving farewell.

Covering

Wood uncovered by tide: bones
broken, worn, bent. No one

cries. The song of the heron?
Leaves without wind, reeds

which cannot touch. Every surface
must retreat from itself, even water.

On the beach, smooth rock
turns to spiral shells, each empty.

All things pray to be lifted
from what they cover.

From under a green blouse
autumn reveals her fire-bright skin.

Stepmother's Breath

The snow has come. Pines are bowing,
thorns pulled to the ground. Deer on the field's edge
disappear. The landing of each flake

a sound like water far from shore
when there is no boat and no wind, only
the stirrings of the current and the brush

against the floor. All fields are palates,
and the world is alien. I pretend to be
without past, without self, waiting for the slow

white to come, for wind to bury me. On morning
there is a lightening of the storm's edge along the hilltops;
an idea of brightness behind a dark curtain.

Everything which has gone into the storm has come out
a stranger to itself. I cannot see the boy I sent
to become who I am. Now, there is only the shape
of something hard beneath a drifting outline.

Birthing

Already I know when I get home
the wind will have taken the autumn leaves,
the long grasses will have been bent
and browned, the ground slick
and muddy, swamps will begin to freeze.

Still, I want to tell myself the story of summer
there as well, of the heavy wet heat and the swollen
boards of the gray porch, the sting of the sweat bee,
the smell of hay and wood and in the evening
the flies above the creek and the dances they do

to draw the trout up from the bends and blow-downs,
the stillness of the late air, the sounds of dark fading
onto the hills and from the sky even then, in its last
breath of day, the color of something as it is born;
bloodied and beautiful and burning.

Who Can Not Return

My father's house has floorboards as wide as a man
and red, cut from massive pines by hand—
uneven, rough-hewn, pegged but tightly bound.
After so many years beneath a ragged carpet
at night they hum and sing and push the light of the moon.

Across the road a cemetery with one stone proclaiming
BLOOM and the broken stubs of others fading
into the ground, the square limestone wall falling
with no one to gather and re-stack it, no one
but the honeysuckle and the roses, wild.

The barn foundation still stands, the scars where
the elms stood, the creek and the logging roads.
Even now in winter the frost heaves relics
from the yard and spring finds them—
the lost ice saw, a milking stool.

The men cannot return. Albert. Bill. Charlie.
Now my brother wakes in the morning alone
beside his dog. Three hundred miles to the east
the ocean spits and blows behind me. Still,
for one moment before I smell the salt, I hear

the waving of the lilac tree against the windows,
or the sound of a man downstairs in the kitchen
cooking breakfast for his sons, and the turning of the
apples in the yard from green to yellow to red.

The Porch We Built

I plumbed posts with lead weight and line;
it was hot and someone kept telling me
to put on a shirt. I felt among the men
of my family; swinging a hammer
and wrestling field stones into place as though
I *were* one of them. I admired the muscle
of their forearms and the guttural sounds they made
as they hefted cement bags, four-by-fours.
In the yard stumps of elms still stood, my great
grandfather walked without canes back and forth
between house and barn, carrying lighter
loads of nails and shovels. At noon I fetched beer
from the sweating kitchen and tried a swallow
of cream ale. Birds in tight formation swooped
across fields, and back then you could still
see the diversion ditch on the side of the hill
and below it the alder swamp with its hidden
trout holes. Each man seemed a giant to me
and all I ever aspired to be was one of them:
hard-handed men who knew how to
throw bales to the top of a loaded wagon
and level a nail with two full swings.

Now the concrete steps are crumbling,
gray wood bends and moans from
the weight of me. I will never be a man who
uses his hands like my brother, or my grandfather.

Still, I am among those who have survived,
and here at the bottom of the valley I am sure
they would do no more than I—sitting in
a lazy chair, watching the tall grasses bend
in a sort of rhythm, the sun fading behind
the house, calling out as they appear: *black locust,*
bluebird, red-tailed hawk, white-tailed deer.
Tonight there will be fireflies as numerous
as the stars, and before morning they too
will turn out their brilliant bodies.

What I Remember

Through windows a still life forms
of rivers and summer grass bending in unison,
of trees turning from red and yellow to bare
to green.

       There was a moment when everything
(cold mornings before the fire started
the sound of the woods before first light in spring
snow and wind and the tin roof collapsing)
became a series of images a life passes on
to no one.

       I realize I do not remember
most of my life, not the best parts or the worst
but just the way things looked at certain times—
the gnarled gray bark of the locust
and the black thorns as they stayed in my hand;
pussy willow curling over stream beds and wind
dipping the soft buds into gathering water.

One evening on the hill above the honey
hives, holding the timothy in my teeth,
watching bees turning in lazy circles turn
into the beat of fireflies—lying down
to sleep, the ground still warm beneath me,
and thinking about the day before,
which had gone as quickly as I had
out into the hills, and had not come back.

Dead Raccoon on I-87

The way he had rolled to the wide, gray shoulder
made me think of laughter, his masked head
tilted back, mouth open, his splayed fingers
held out as if in protest of uproarious guffaws,
his bloated body looking as though he were
about to expel the air all at once, or perhaps
struggling to get enough between chortles.

Crows danced to either side as other,
wider wings circled overhead. Certainly
there was music, in passing. Perhaps he had led
the perfect life; scrounging the borders of
the city, peeling back the lids of municipal
dumpsters. Perhaps now he finally has
his banded arms around the great hot dog
in the sky, and it is I who am the fool.
After all, what better way to leave than
displayed in fine form for the constant
admiration of the morning commuters?
And what worse way to continue, than
among them?

Grace

I spent all day walking ridges, above me limbs
holding a cloudless sky like tangled pillars
and slanted ground pulling towards the river,
tiny gorges hidden in thick folds. My feet rose
and fell as if all breath were one: heaving earth
and tossing leaves, turning stars some hours yet to come.

There was devil's paintbrush and buttercup and spring cress
and blackberry blossoms. I read once that when something is beautiful
we do not have the grace to leave it, and I stayed as long
as I could—until the dog got nervous and whined and there was
nothing for it but to walk up and over the hill, where a long barn
waited, and the house, and I knew I had spent what grace was allotted
me all in one place, in one afternoon, and I could never tell it
as it was. No one had seen me as I was except the sun,
and the trunks of trees, and the grass, and the dog.

Untitled

I dreamt I was in high school: a star on the football
field and with a certain girl who could not keep her
hands off me. But I itched, inside. I could not stay
in the sunned parking lot to speak as a young man would—

    I noticed behind the school a dimness,
and I was pulled towards it; first walking and then
as I moved into the thin grass of the practice fields
I hunched until my knuckles became feet and I grunted
as a primate.

    In the distance I could see outlines of
those now dead, but the air thickened and each
snuffling half-step grew in viscus resistance.
I turned back but a storm brewed, funnels of black wind
poured from the hills.

    I could hear the river calling,
the gnarled limbs of submerged trees snagging the water,
mud in slides from each bank. A deer: bent wrongly, bloated,
floating. The waning moon came for me and I drowned
in the bright lunar waters.

    My last thought was of my unborn
son and would I, in an afterlife, get to meet children I did not have?
Then the light split me in half horizontal; it was the morning
sun as it pried the lids of my eyes open . . . my bed
seemed a pool and all around

    birds of morning
made what noises they do when there is nothing for them
but the rise of day, and the struggle of living ahead.

The Last Day

That morning I helped with chores—
shoveling shit, spreading hay, carrying
white pails of water to the stalls. The long
rows were full of high-backed hogs
and at the far end of the barn piglets
ran in open pens before we gathered them
to trim their teeth and remove what parts
make other hogs. I knew so little I felt as if
I knew all there was to know; I scooped whey
and corn and grain and brushed horses and
put a steel machine to milking.
Mike had gone to run the spreader
and told me to come find him
when men came to take the old horse
because she was big and spooked easy
and did not like the dark mouth of the trailer.
They came while I was in the loft and too late
I realized they had already begun
and were having a bad time of it.
She was half again as old as I was
but just then, as she loosed a metal
door from it hinges and rose onto two legs
I saw the full length of her, and the day
seemed much shorter as I saw
how it could be the last day for the two
men who had come to take her away
and I saw also how I had failed her

in the last moments she needed me;
to be sent into the unknown by
the voice of the farm hand who had
fed and saddled and spoken kind words
to her, to have faced strange men and the
darkness of what lay in front of her
with a familiar hand on her dark mane
might have been the only truly kind
thing I had in my power to do. I ran
the hill and found Mike but it was too
late, I heard the rifle make its final protest
and there was no pretending about it.
It was my fault, he said. *It was my job
and I left it to you and I shouldn't have.*
I know now at least that I can never
repay her. I know about the finality
of failure. I know about last days
and how we only ever get one of them.

Quarry Man, Roma

On working days we would ride high on the back of the truck
leaning over the cab and feeling as strong as we were, pulling
hard on our bodies to load and shovel, break and stack, it seemed
we could never run out, and on cold days we worked right through
lunch to hop off early before it got too dark, and my baby and me
we could go all night at the bar and then some. I played a little harp
and she could swing and dance and make her hair lift in halos,
the music was in her and out of her in ways that made me feel sometimes
like I was seeing the bright fire of creation, like God must have
when he made Eve, the world was at once dimmer in contrast and even
the darkness jumped, towards her and away again as the men lit
smokes and the lights swung from fixtures in the wind a body makes
as it moves, and she burned and burned all night and we boys
held our moth bodies near as we could, cashing in hour by hour
the day for another bottle in the hopes it would pass her lips,
and it did, and everyone always said I knew her like no one
else, I knew when she had had enough to drink, when to take
her home and when to stand aside and let her breathe fury
into the crowd. I knew she had inside her an anger which twisted
and pulled and caught itself up in the smoke and tar and
whiskey and heroin, they told me I knew her and I was there
when they brought my baby out in the black bag.

The Welder's Daughter

       I know now about the morning,
how its ghosts run from east in lengthening shadows,
about how the sky might fall not in pieces but whole,
swallowing ground and water and light.

I know now what happened to the welder's daughter
who disappeared last fall, how she walked toward the lake
seeing for a moment the face of her mother, chin down,
turning away, how it felt to be suddenly not alone again,
and then the calm call of rhythm and wave, the first step
on the slick rocks, wings spreading out behind her
and then flight, freedom, the cold.

Cutting Ice, 1841

When we came down the hill we had the ice sleigh
loaded full and it was slick and cold enough so the horses
kept stamping their feet and the snow didn't melt an inch
even with the cloudless sky pouring out above us
blue and light and the water we revealed square by square
shone back at us and we were blinded all day. It was clear
and sharp and while we loaded up the runners froze so bad
it took the maul to get them free, and so when we came
down the hill towards the house, the horses might have been
a little too eager to get warm again or maybe we just didn't
see it right: the way the bank cuts away against the hill
and the spillway stream was fifty feet below and frozen.
We hit it wrong and she slid over the edge and caught
a hemlock but not before Jonah fell the whole way and the
ice of the stream split his head like a berry. I saw him tumble
all the way down but out of the corner of my eye so that for
a minute I thought the earth just came out from under him
and I guess in a way it did, and then I remember looking down
and Pa running and sliding down after him and the blood
sliding down over the frozen waterfall and catching
in the cold, and then stopping, and then we all stopped,
and then we couldn't, and we righted the sleigh and came
back to the house with only five good pieces and what used to be
my brother, and they were by then both as cold as the other.

My Lands Are Where My Dead Lie Buried

In South Dakota they told me you could watch
your dog run away for three days. There was a fire
on the prairie—from the highway I could see
black sky raising like hackles. I fled
the hills and headed east passed the bed of a sea;
at night there were no eyes along the road. I saw
nothing that lived for a whole day except cars
and a gas station and an empty hotel. I dreamt
of trees speaking in low voices along the edges
of a river, moving a bundle wrapped in cloth
between leaved hands. In Mitchell I was cornered
by wrestlers in a townie bar. We compared scars and ears
and just before dawn they carried me like a corpse
to my room with a golf club and a picture of Rushmore.
I woke feeling as if I had missed something, maybe
back in the trenches of the badlands, or as though
the Ponderosa back west would die if I left.
It has been several years, and no word from them.
None of it was a dream. I lost the pictures but
I remember my hands along the top of the grass
and the hills in my rear view, imagining a dog with Crazy Horse,
the three of us pining for the prairie, still visible through the smoke.

Good Boy

This year for Christmas a friend brought over his dog
who was to be put down the next week (tumors spread from
his leg, which was frozen, up to his lungs, which gasped) and
the fucking thing wagged its tail and looked so goddamn
happy the whole time, just to be at the party where we were all
yelling merry Christmas and trying not to stare at its swollen leg
and drinking a lot. Later in the night we went into the creek
even though it was eight degrees out and the ice was forming
on the sloped bank and the water was deeper than normal
because of the recent snow and we all ran and screamed and ran
and someone asked me later why the hell would you do something
like that, run from a perfectly good and warm house into a frozen
creek to swim at two in the morning on Christmas and I thought
because I won't be at the party where everyone says goodbye to me
and my frozen whatever from the tumors or maybe I just die in a car
accident I won't ever wag my tail and be happy to be dying
so this is it, right now, when my feet are bleeding
and my balls are up in my throat and my skin is pink as a baby
but goddamn if I ain't grinning like I just learned I had a son.
And no one will have to pretend, at that future party, that it is not
shitty as hell to hurt or drink or die. But we were alive, and we wanted
to know it, and every time we could prove it to ourselves, even on
Christmas Eve, even with the cold and the dying dog, we did.

The Time a Man Thought I Was a Deer

Maybe it was the steam of my breath
which gave me away. In the air
bullets sound like a high whine or whistle
that might have come from within,
like screams made from
a long way off.

My grandfather told me you don't hear
the ones that hit you. He had one less
arm than me but one more war.
I picture him skinny and young and driving
a tractor through the orchard, the way my
grandmother describes the day she first saw him.
I never asked her to tell me about the last day.
Somewhere in that orchard are things we both have lost.
The sounds of the apples falling. The pasture emptying
of cows and on each swaying hip the flies dancing
away from the lash of the tail.

What I Saw

Plates scattered with the ash of a few
hundred cigarettes, brown bottoms
falling over one another as legs in a mass grave.
Everywhere bottles with the liquor gone
and now carrying some small part of his lips.
Bits of food; crumbs, here or there
a bone, the black residue of condiments gathering
nervous swarms of insects which lifted on clear
wings and settled again from time to time. Flies
made a home too, on his mouth. In it. When they
rose in unison I thought he might have spoken.
One lid hung open, and I remember sometimes
before sleep the way an eye looks
when it no longer sees—as if the world were
unsurprising, colorless, static. I will not
speak of the smell. Only his hands looked
the same, one caught on the taut loop a belt
pushed against, the other reaching still
towards the brown, mottled carpet,
and the upright beer can; red and catching
the fractured sun from the blinds, throwing
it out again to dance against the flat walls.

As I Remember It

We had been at a party,
it was late, his car was
on the side of the road. It was bad
but not that bad. Ruined tires,
damaged side, but basically
intact. Not even a shattered window.

We called his phone and called his
name but I figured he had been drinking
and had a friend pick him up. His girlfriend
and the sheriff had come
and they yelled too, but,
nothing.

He hanged himself with his tie
from the branches of a tree
not 200 yards away.
I found out he died
right about the time we
were calling. I must have
just missed him.

The leaves blew in dry piles along the side of the road;
I could hear them all night on the broken pavement
and the ditches, and the branches, filling with autumn.

Great Blue Heron

I picked a careful footing
between granite shards and dead oak leaves
as around me bare branches began to reach
one fraction further towards the sun. Below
a dark shape—a great blue heron
as it lifted over the water and for a moment
beneath was still, the geese quieted,
and slowly I felt I was in the wake of something
I had caused, something almost without movement,
almost without sound, broken now into fading
ripples in tall pond grass, cattails, then nothing
more than reflection of sky almost without clouds.

Mountain, Thursday

My phone rang and it was Stella calling because she
missed Ruth and she knew I missed Ruth also and because
my father was her brother and we both missed him
and it was a hard day to be missing someone, a Thursday
when the rest of the world was away at work
and the emptiness of a house could overwhelm—

out any window might be the yard
from when you were a girl and the tree might be
the maple you sat under when the sun was hottest
and the sounds of your mother came from the house;
a call which at any other time might have been
annoyance or anger but now was the thing
you wanted to hear so badly you would trade
all the white laced windows and the stacks of books
and the old farm itself to hear it one more time,
sounds that will never come to you again
in just that way but which might on the right
kind of day some time from now pass from you.

I looked up and saw the weather had moved in
and the mountain was an island which sank
stone by stone into wind and water. I told
her it did not get easier for me but that I
understood I needed to get better
and then I hung up and put my feet on the
wet snow and if I had been able I might have
risen with the clouds towards whatever
passes for forever here, in the world where
not a single day is safe from death.

Botanical Gardens Beach, Vancouver Island

There was a sign: *beware of rogue waves*
and below it a candle and a shirt and a few
shells arraigned just so—we were there
to sit with them in remembrance.

There had been a storm and a neap tide
and above the tidal pools where trees
dipped coiled ankles of root in the pacific
long kelp bodies lay with driftwood
lifted from the water, aliens in a place
unimaginable to the feeding urchins, limp
and hollow and asleep on the black rock.

Beyond them a small cliff, overhung with fir
and moss and the waves reaching white tongues
to its curved body, pulling small and perfect circles
out of the stone; muscles packed in lonely cities
lined with sea grass; something volcanic having
drowned here, something of heat having quenched itself.

It seemed to me the best kind of place to have died,
where water and land remembered each other and wore
away their disagreements, where the road ends
and the human voices fall into the breathing sea.
A good place to be carried from, to be swept off your
feet and away to where they would no longer
be used for standing. To let life be taken
from you by waves so wild they are called rogues
and placed far out to sea, where the slow dance
of the kelp still mesmerizes, where there is current
and motion and rhythm and the unending blood of the world.

Small Coyote, Trap

On the way home this year I took a back road
I had not driven before. The highway sagged
and along the edges, the blacktop spider-webbed
and the shoulders pulled away into the dirt.
I passed a pond and beside it in the snow
something red. It was late afternoon in November
and dusk settled in on the tops of bare trees, from the south
and west the light bent, I could not see in my mirror
what it was. I remember walking in the shallow snow
and coming along beside the wide circle of blood.
I've heard it said that a body cannot be still in great pain,
but no part of him moved except his eyes.
For a long while we could only watch and beg.
He could not grant my wish: to rise and walk
into the pines. I granted his, after a time. When
it was done I wiped my boots on the flat oak leaves
so that he would not stain the black rug of my car.

Untitled

For Sharon

How could we have seen,
on the day we wed, I would
later fade into the back room
and be unable to attend even
the cows?

You were so beautiful,
and now I have had to leave you
as my arm left me so many years
before. I know how long days can be
when the pain of something is
as a ghost: hollow, empty, receding
but never gone.

Our daughters work the barns.
Though I will not see the fruit of
their labor, I am never far. Each
time a wet birth bloods the hay
or as day begins some work
which must be done calls, it will
be as if I am there.

Morning. Meet me
in the kitchen as we always did:
each moment bridled with promise
of day lain out before it. Coffee,
light, smoke, our children, forever.

The Girl with the Bike

I always wanted to love a woman like you, a relationship
which for a while was full of conversation about culture
and society and great sex and a motorcycle and which ends
with you just leaving one morning while I slept, and me—
waking in the cool blue of the day before light
and noticing beside me the empty bed and the closet
gasping, open-mouthed, and the sound of your bike
as it rolls down whatever country lane we lived on
for the last time. It would be spring or early summer,
and the day would adorn itself calmly with dew,
the birds would tear themselves into pieces
with a song of normalcy, and I would lie alone,
wondering if, had I never met you, I would be as lonely
as I am which, having never met you, I often wonder now.

Lake, Night

The lake, with moon over easy. Here, a loon
can sing
without repercussion.
An island
with bent pines,
the stone shore pulling
up and away.
How will we know when we have reached the afterlife?
Once, men spoke of angels,
or women
who pulled the dead from battle.
There is no battle
in which the soul is free
from itself. See—
the shore has pursed its lips,
the mountains
cup the stars and the fireflies
with one set of arms.
Where is the howl of the coy dog now?
Beyond stars: Milky Way. Within the water:
only absence, measured.

These Things Too Have Shape

At the base of the pines
mourning doves tug
at a fallen nest.

On the singing lawn of spring
it is a woven brown island.
Before the sun rose,
wind pulled tall branches
in staccato patterns.

From a child's foot
a ball comes. Each a clarion call:
wind, pines, dove, child
above the ball and nest.
Mothers turn their smooth heads.

The Ox and I

Here in a valley of the High Peaks,
leaning against the white rail of a fenced field
which holds a few steers, a bull, a sagging
old ox which has lost its pulling partner
and with nothing to offer as they snort warily
in my direction, nor to fend off the face flies
(my god, someone named them face flies)
which plague their eyes and nose I can only
talk softly to them as if we have some thing
in common we have just now discovered—
the way the leaves turn their heads light and dark
in the wind before a storm, or the movement
of our shadows toward the east until the tips
touch the tree line and the sky begins to bruise
around the edges . . . they know I have much to say:
and here in the house they keep I am free
to say it, though no man can turn his black eyes
on me the way they do. We both know, the ox and I,
which sorts of things will be left behind when
the night bitters and the wolves commence
the dance of forlorn selection. Not us. Not now.
The barn opens the wide smile of doors.

Weight

The buses run and run alongside the trains
and the roads are covered with cars leaving

small bits of their tires behind as letters
on a brittle gray screen of love. Buildings

crowd in on one another in admiration of the
people milling about. Even churches

are in reverence of parishioners, opening
their hollow bodies and filling their chests

with sound before sending the men
and women out into the song-less city.

All the while, the ground admires trees. Even at
night, he feels the pull of them as they bend.

Looking up has taught him what is beneath;
bad dreams filter up from the stone,

and he has learned what is burning is his heart.
To him the season of leaves is the hour

before the season without. Nothing will fall
from him, only to him. *What can they know*

of weight, he thinks. There are no changes.
Each time he turns, the sun is unmoved.

Barns, Owls

The big one fell to a tornado.
Center-cut beams pulled apart at the joints.
The howling wind sounded like
the scream of rabbits, *distress*
my father called it, the sound
before the owl lands.

They lived in the other barn, the one filled with hay.
Between the rafters the round heads turned and noticed
everything, the round faces were not afraid, the round
eyes did not look away. Nothing they did
made sound. Sleeping. Flight. They never spoke.

Now the foundation pulls up a grass blanket
and hunkers into the hard earth. The rotted beams melt.
On nights lit by the moon there is still the passing
shadow, the sound of dead grass, *distress.*

Stabbing, California

I did not see the knife, only a flash
and in the moonlight the sound of tearing
caught me flat footed, I could not place it—

it was his shirt, I think, or his stomach.
All sound died and then came back
in a roar, the peepers a chaotic blast and
caught in the air was gasping and footsteps
in rapid retreat, above us the sky had
lost the stars and struggled with
the bulk of itself, and fell in dark pools
that gathered at my feet.

This kind of night, I thought, could go on forever.
I did not have to look towards the heat in my hands,
I could stare to the sky until the stars revealed themselves.

Belted Kingfisher

Yesterday the belted kingfisher plucked
minnows from a pool beneath the bridge
as I cast under honeysuckle and waved
my arms to make the flies my father tied
dance from rill to rill, air to water.

Much of my time I have spent not moving;
back against a tree in the darkness before first light—
in my hands my grandfather's gun still wound
with electrical tape to hold a broken stock—
waiting for deer or turkeys or squirrels or morning.

I know what hunting is. The long while before the pull
of trigger, when nothing is as it seems—air moving
slowly around languid breath, trees bending, water
pouring down and down, the passing of light from eye
to eye, the sense of things as they are when nothing
is watching them. Then is the moment before:
the kingfisher dipping above streams, movement
which puts the body in a line *just so*, the will to strike.

What I Have Not Told The Hemlock

On certain days when the snow is especially heavy
or deep or the wind is bad or on nights without moon
where clouds simmer on the fire of stars
I have an agreement with the hemlock

who lowers his shoulders and hands me a few branches—
and I admit the flat short needles scratch my skin,
my arms grow tired quickly and I must sit to hold
so much but I begin to see: the slow walk of the
stones down the hillside towards the creek
and the swaying of water up and down with rain
and seasons as they melt from one to another

through the green skinned moss the belly of
the fallen oak turns to dirt and then we agree
the hemlock and I to never speak of these things
as I hand him back his arms and teeth and even
now he and I both know nothing I have said
will convey it, nothing we have shared can be given
by only the sounds of words in the halls of the mind.